CRISIS
OR
CONFERENCE!

CRISIS

OR

CONFERENCE!

A Master List for Conference Planners

Tony Carey

THE INDUSTRIAL SOCIETY
and
STIRLING USA

First published 1997 by
The Industrial Society
Robert Hyde House
48 Bryanston Square
London W1H 7LN

Stirling
22883 Quicksilver Drive
Stirling VA
USA

ISBN 1 85835 463 3

British Library Cataloguing-in-Publication Data. A
Catalogue record for this book is available from the
British Library.

Typeset by: Cheryl Zimmerman
Printed by: Lavenham Press
Cover design: Rhodes Design

The Industrial Society is a registered charity no. 290003.

CONTENTS

LAYOUT AND NOTATION SYSTEM

The Checklists in this Guide are printed on the left-hand page. Numbers at the end of the items refer to the relevant, explanatory 'footnotes' on the facing page.

In some cases notes of a general nature have been included on the right hand page. Where they do not refer to a specific list item, they are annotated by bullet points.

INTRODUCTION

When I first found myself, almost by accident, working as a full-time conference organiser in the late 1970s, I looked for a training course to provide me with a basic grounding in the skills of the job. Apart from a one week programme run by The International Association of Professional Conference Organisers (IAPCO) in Switzerland, none seemed to exist. So, in 1985, by now a slightly less naive event manager, I set up a short residential course entitled: "An Introduction To Conference Management" using friendly experts in the business as tutors.

It proved successful and people signed up for it from all over Europe and as far away as Singapore. Many companies that sent delegates on those early courses are still doing so.

One of the more popular features of the course proved to be the checklists which formed a series of aides memoire for the instruction.

This book represents a decade of distillation of those checklists. It is not all my own work. Over the years, generations of delegates to my courses have contributed ideas and personal experiences which I have incorporated into the lists. I am indebted to them.

Conference organising is largely a matter of common sense, fore-thought, attention to detail, team work and sometimes crisis management, but few of us have the ability to keep in our minds the 1001 important things that require attention and decision.

The purpose of this book is to make the task of the event planner less a test of memory. If it saves you a few hours work and a few £'s, I will be satisfied.

I have designed the book to be pocket or handbag friendly so that you can take it on site visits and I have written it so that the complete beginner and the more experienced practitioner will find it useful.

You may find that some lists contain ideas that have no application to your event. This is inevitable because of the diversity of meetings that are held. A suggestion that applies to an association convention may have little relevance when you are organising a training course for 15 or a sales conference for 150.

Association events can make demands not found in the corporate sector which in turn have no relevance to the organiser of a speculative event. I have tried to cover all the angles.

I hope that this book will prove useful not just to the professional organiser, but also to the General, Sales and Banqueting managers of conference hotels who will, I hope, derive an insight into their client's needs, (and may use it to help those clients who have failed to obtain their own copy). For similar reasons, Convention Bureau staff may also find it helpful.

Primarily, I hope that it will prove invaluable to those who are suddenly called upon to organise an event and wonder where to start.

I do not pretend that the lists are exhaustive and you will see that, where possible, space has been allocated for personal notes and additions. In any case, we all have our own approach to the business of event organising.

A word to the novice conference organiser. Despite the length and apparent complexity of this Guide do not be intimidated! Because I have tried to cover the demands of every type of event, it is more comprehensive than you will initially need but I hope you will continue to find it an invaluable source of reference as you gain experience.

I regret that space does not allow me to extol the pleasures and rewards enjoyed by the successful conference organiser. It is an activity that can become addictive if, like me, you relish the challenge of creating a congenial team able to turn an idea into a stimulating, enjoyable and successful event.

In the European conference industry we owe much to our counterparts in North America who have refined the necessary skills and developed the business to the relatively sophisticated state it is in today. For this reason, I have included a glossary of terms at the end of the book showing differences in terminology between Europe and North America.

For anyone making a career in this business, I commend membership of Meeting Professionals International. Based in Dallas, Texas, MPI is the world's largest professional association for people working in the meetings industry, with over 14,000 members in 45 countries. It exists to promote conferences as a form of communication and to encourage excellence in this specialised field through education and networking. MPI's 'Certificate in Meeting Management' (CMM), has become a much sought after professional qualification.

I am deeply grateful to all those who have encouraged me to prepare this work for publication and have helped with advice and proof reading, especially:

Jim Fausel
Peter Haigh
Shirley Hamill
Louise Roos
Terry Thiessen
Vanessa Woodbine-Parish

My sincere thanks, also, to my secretary Ali Le Ray who has endured innumerable drafts and to my wife Barbara without whose encouragement, I would still be dreaming about it.

Finally, I welcome comments and suggestions from readers about this work and can be reached by e-mail on: **tonyccma@itl.net**

Tony Carey, CMM

PREFACE

Surveys have shown that the conference industry in the UK is worth in the region of £6 billion per year ($20.6 billion in the US) which gives some indication of the importance – and popularity – of this means of communication.

In the last few years, organisations have come to appreciate the potency of a well-staged meeting and are investing increased resources in professional planning, presentation and analysis of their events. For example, executives now take for granted that the social and recreational elements of a conference programme can be as important as the overtly educational sessions. The principles of adult learning have passed from the world of academia to the field of business.

It is generally accepted that a meeting or conference which fulfils its objectives is not only a useful management resource, but also an important part of the communications spectrum.

Unfortunately, too many senior executives still fail to appreciate that successful conference management is much more than a series of administrative and logistic procedures.

Whatever its objectives, a meeting will never realise its potential if the organiser fails to understand the needs of the stake-holders, if he or she cannot create and lead an ad hoc team and, most importantly, if the planning is devoid of creative thought. Administrative perfection is vital but it is not enough.

The qualities which the most successful meeting planners bring to the task are a rare mixture and deserve more recognition than they usually receive.

PART ONE: PRE-PLANNING

Introduction

When one is first presented with the prospect of organising a conference or meeting, there is a temptation to rush off and find a venue and then to fit everything into it. A better tactic is to sit down and make a note of all the things you need to know about the event.

I call this pre-planning. It involves research and thinking into the scope of the project. Now is the time to start building up a library of information and references. Since ideas and questions will occur to you when you least expect them, it may be worth carrying a small dictaphone around with you.

1.1 PRINCIPLES OF SUCCESSFUL CONFERENCE PLANNING

Principles are generally dry, theoretical ideas more often applied by accident than by design. As a basis for discussion, here are my top ten principles of successful conference planning.

1. The establishment and maintenance of a clear aim[1]

2. An understanding of the needs and expectations of your delegates both individually and in a group[2]

3. Meticulous planning and preparation[3]

4. The formulation of a stimulating and balance programme appropriate to the objectives, the delegates and the location[4]

5. The choice of a suitable venue in an appropriate location[5]

6. Thorough budgetary planning and control[6]

7. Clear and timely communication vertically and horizontally[7]

8. The creation of a motivated management team to which responsibility can be successfully delegated

9. Simple administrative procedures

10. The projection of a suitable image to participants and to the public

1.1 NOTES ON PRINCIPLES OF SUCCESSFUL CONFERENCE PLANNING

1. If you don't know what you're trying to achieve you'll never achieve it.

2. See Delegate Profile (page 12).

3. See The Components of Planning (page 4).

4. See Planning Programmes (page 42).

5. See Sources of Reference (page 16).

6. See Budget for IT (page 36).

7. See The Decision Hedgehog (page 64).

1.2 THE COMPONENTS OF PLANNING

All tasks become easier when they are broken down into their component parts. Event planning is no exception. The multitude of activities and actions may be divided up in a number of ways. Here is a suggestion for your 'Action Plan'.[1]

1. Pre-planning. This includes:
- Setting objectives
- Creating a team
- Preparing a Meeting Profile
- Preparing a Delegate Profile
- Establishing operating systems
- Establishing lines of communication
- Preparing an 'Action Schedule'[2]
- Setting financial parameters
- Arranging briefings
- Committing all decisions to paper and disseminating them

2. Planning. This might include:
- An outline event programme
- Venue selection and liaison plan
- Supplier lists
- Cash flow forecasts
- Marketing plan
- Print and publication schedule
- Accommodation plan
- Travel plan
- List of legal considerations
- List of financial considerations
- Speaker, presenter lists
- Food and beverage plan
- Social events plan
- Recreation plan
- Recce and rehearsal plan
- PR plan
- Event evaluation system[3]
- Contingency plans
- 'Enhancements' list[4]
- VIP handling plan
- 'Miscellaneous matters' list
- Post event plan

1.2 NOTES ON THE COMPONENTS OF PLANNING

1. In some quarters, this is put together into a single document and called a Business Plan. Whatever you call it, this compendium of tasks should become the project bible to which everyone will refer. As it will be subject to amendment, a loose-leaf or computer format is recommended.

2. All tasks listed in this schedule should be given an 'action by' date and the name of the person responsible.

3. You should devise a method to quantify the success of your conference.

4. Enhancements are those creative extras and bright ideas that will give the event your personal hallmark.

• Planners should adopt their own systems for drawing together the many strands of an event.

• An alternative (or additional) aid to planning is a computer Flow Chart listing tasks against time. Software programmes are available.

"Plans get you into things but you got to work your way out."

Will Rogers, 1949

1.3 PRE-PLANNING – GENERAL

When the Chief Executive of your organisation says: "I want you to run a conference" you will need to know certain things before you even start thinking about it. Here are some questions you might ask him or her.

- Whose conference is it?[1]

- To whom do I report?

- Who is the final decision-taker?

- How much authority do I have?[2]

- What is the aim of the event?[3]

- What are the time parameters?[4]

- What are the geographical constraints?[5]

- Who is funding the event?[6]

- What is the budget?

- Who are the delegates and where will they be travelling from?[7]

- How many delegates are likely or possible?

- Has the event been held before? If so, where?[8]

- What mandatory requirements are being imposed on the event?[9]

- Is there an associated exhibition?

- What is format and duration?

- Is a post event report required?

1.3 NOTES TO PRE-PLANNING – GENERAL

1. The answer to the first three questions may be the same person or, in some large organisations, different people. It is vital to establish the chain of responsibility at the outset.

2. Regarding venue and speaker selection, for instance.

3. Beware multiple objectives.

4. What are the earliest and latest dates the event could be staged.

5. Should you be looking at city or country or airport locations, at home or abroad?

6. In other words: who has a stake in its success? And will the attendees be paying?

7. Also ask about partners.

8. If so, you have a useful reference.

9. E.g. Is the Chairman insisting on an adjacent golf course.

"A good beginning makes a good ending"

English proverb

1.4 PRE-PLANNING – FINANCIAL

Fired with enthusiasm and equipped with a clear brief, you will need to make one more appointment before planning starts in earnest. Your conference initiator may not be the same person who controls the budget. It is important to have clear financial guidelines at the outset. Here are some questions that you might ask the Budget Controller.

- What is the budget for the event?[1]

- How is the budget to be divided up?[2]

- What does the budget include or exclude?[3]

- When is the money available?

- Can income be generated?[4]

- By when must all accounts be paid ?[5]

- Who will approve or audit the accounts?

- In which currency should accounts be kept?

- In what form should the accounts be presented?[6]

- When is the final account required?

- What supplier restraints exist?[7]

- Is there a contingency allowance?[8]

- Does the event have an income/expenditure history?[9]

1.4 NOTES ON PRE-PLANNING - FINANCIAL

1. This should be the same as your original brief!

2. Are there set amounts for accommodation or audio-visual, for example.

3. E.g. Delegate travel, PR, print, insurance.

4. E.g. Sponsorship.

5. The organisation's financial year end and other factors may determine when monies will be paid out.

6. Chat to your accounts department early on (good PR) and seek their advice. Their response will dictate how suppliers present their invoices, etc.

7. E.g. Your organisation may have agreements with airlines and insist you use them. (Thus influencing your choice of destination.)

8. This is a bit presumptuous, but most budget controllers allow a flexibility factor. Knowing what it is will reduce your stress levels when an emergency occurs.

9. Your budgeting will be made easier if you know what has been spent on what in the past.

I once heard of an independent conference organiser who ran a major event for a corporate client and submitted his invoice within the agreed budget. Surprisingly, the client told him to add a further 10% to the bill because to come in on budget would cause his Financial Controller to reduce the conference budget in the following year.

1.5 AN EVENT PROFILE

Every member of your organising team and every supplier needs some basic information about the event if they are to commit to it. You will find it useful to prepare certain briefing documents. The first of these is an event profile.

This should include:

- The title of the meeting

- The name of the organiser

- The name of the organisation for whom it is being run[1]

- Addresses and contact numbers for the above[1]

- The aim of the event

- A brief outline of the event[2]

- The dates and duration of the event[3]

- Maximum and minimum numbers of
    - delegates
    - partners
    - staff
    - guests
    - customers/clients

- The proposed location

- The venue (when known)

- Budget factors

- Other planning factors[4]

- An outline programme

1.5 NOTES ON AN EVENT PROFILE

1. This may be a department or a client.

2. No more than one sentence. E.g. "A meeting to acquaint our sales force about the new advertising campaign".

3. It may be helpful to indicate which parameters are not inflexible.

4. These might include cultural factors, the presence of a VIP or unique production facilities.

- Normally, it will be helpful to attach a 'Delegate Profile' to the Event Profile (see list 1.6).

- The Event Profile should be distributed on a very wide scale, vertically and horizontally throughout participating organisations.

- The Event Profile should not be confused with a 'Bid Document' or 'Request for Proposals' (RFP), although the two have similarities, they serve different purposes. The former imparts information, the latter solicits information.

- Some of the details on your Event Profile may change, (e.g. numbers) so it should be dated. Subsequent, updated editions might be printed on coloured paper.

"It is a bad plan that admits of no modification"

Publilius Syrus, 1st Century BC

1.6 DELEGATE PROFILE

Needless to say, delegates come in all shapes and sizes, but at most events there are common denominators even it is only their mutual interest in the subject. Your suppliers will be better able to fulfil delegate needs if they have an understanding of the sort of people who are attending the event. So a Delegate Profile can save you a lot of explaining. It might include the following information about attendees:

- Average age of delegates[1]

- Ratio of the sexes

- Their places of origin[2]

- Management level[3]

- Their occupations[4]

- Whether they know each other[5]

- What factors unite them[6]

- Any distinctive preferences or distinguishing characteristics[7]

- Their level of experience of the meeting subject

- The main reasons for their attendance[8]

- The potential level of spend at the venue[9]

- Languages

1.6 NOTES ON DELEGATE PROFILE

● Not all of these items will be appropriate.

1. Possibly include the age range.

2. I.e. Where they have travelled from or the main countries of origin.

3. This will tell you something about their expectations.

4. White or blue collar, business or artisan.

5. This will influence your work and social programmes.

6. Work or leisure interests, perhaps.

7. E.g. Cultural, religious, political or language.

8. Is attendance compulsory?

9. Include their discretionery spend on beverages, gifts, taxis, etc.

People have often been likened to snowflakes. This analogy is meant to suggest that each is unique – no two alike. This is quite patently not the case. People are quite simply a dime a dozen. And, I hasten to add, their only similarity to snowflakes resides in their invariable and lamentable tendency to turn, in a few warm days, to slush.

Fran Lebowitz, 1981

1.7 HELP FROM A CONVENTION AND VISITORS BUREAU

Most cities and regions, if they are serious about attracting conference business, have a Convention and Visitor Bureau (CVB), although it may operate under a different name such as Tourist Office.

They exist to encourage you to choose their locality, to help you find a suitable venue and to make the most of your conference visit, so that you will return.

CVBs are an invaluable source of assistance and listed here are some of the products and services that they may be able to provide.

- Assistance and advice

- Information material
  - Hotel directories
  - Area guides
  - Convention centre details

- Calendars
  - Of local events [1]
  - Of visiting conferences [2]

- Coordination
  - with civic authorities
  - with tourist facilities
  - with other planners

- Guidance
  - On local conditions [3]
  - Entertainment
  - Local speakers
  - Transport

- Introductions to and lists of:
  - Suppliers
  - Carriers
  - Past events [4]

- Marketing material, such as:
  - Shell brochures [5]
  - Slides
  - Posters
  - Videos

- Local media introductions

- Site inspections (and flights)

- Civic hospitality

- Free entry to civic attractions

- Sponsorship

1.7 NOTES ON HELP FROM A CONVENTION AND VISITORS BUREAU

1. Useful so that you can choose to avoid, or possibly coincide with major festivals, trades fairs, etc.

2. You may wish to liaise with meetings planned immediately before or after yours.

3. It is vital to tap into this source of knowledge if disasters are to be foreseen.

4. Useful for references.

5. These are pictorial promotional brochures, without copy, on which clients may overprint.

• As CVBs are funded either by their local authority or their members, their recommendations have to be impartial.

"If you are looking for a new destination may we give you a totally unbiased recommendation — Malta."

Letter from the Malta National Tourist Office

1.8 SOURCES OF REFERENCE FOR VENUE SEEKERS

The past ten years has seen a considerable increase in the number of conference venues available to an event organiser. These sources of reference may help you to find the right one.

- Printed venue directories
- Venue directories on disk or CD ROM
- Venue finding agencies
- Conference management agencies
- Destination management companies
- Travel agents
- Conference industry associations
- Production companies
- The Internet
- Hotel group central reservation offices
- Convention and Visitor Bureaux
- Tourist offices (National/regional)
- Airlines
- Yellow pages
- Public libraries
- TV travel programmes
- Travel guides
- Trade exhibitions
- Trade magazines
- Incoming mail
- Local offices of your own organisation
- Hotel guides
- Your own files
- Other departments of your organisation
- Familiarisation visits
- Hotel placement services
- Colleagues

1.8 NOTES ON SOURCES OF REFERENCE FOR VENUE SEEKERS

- There's no shortage of free advice in the meetings business, especially when it comes to venue finding. But how much of it is totally impartial?

- Most of the sources on the left have an axe to grind and a cynic might suggest that:

  - Directories won't list places that haven't paid to be included.

  - Associations are pledged to promote their own members.

  - Agencies recommend most highly those venues that pay them a commission.

  - CVBs are limited by their geographical/ political boundaries.

  - Magazines have a tendency to feature their advertisers.

  - Hotel groups only promote their own members.

  - Airlines have links with specific hotels in most destinations.

- Usually, the best sources of advice are your colleagues in the business. This explains why networking is such a valued management tool in the conference industry.

"Never ask of him who has, but of him who wishes you well."

Spanish proverb

1.9 VENUE SELECTION PROCEDURE

There is no such place as the ideal venue this side of paradise. Finding the best is usually a question of compromise. It helps to have a standard procedure to follow.

- Consider the aim of the event

- Re-read your Delegate Profile

- Decide what attributes the destination must have and those which it should have[1]

- Eliminate those regions and destinations that are outside the frame

- Decide on the style of venue best suited to your event[2]

- Prepare and despatch a Bid Document to a list of destination CVBs[3]

- Collate the information received and reduce your list of destinations

- Shortlist the possible venues and request conference packs and availability states[4]

- Compare venue facilities against your list of essential and preferred needs

- Decide the locality and further reduce your shortlist of venues to a maximum of three

- Obtain references

- Visit these venues[5]

- Enter first round of negotiation[6]

- Make a provisional choice[7]

- Re-visit your chosen venue and enter second round of negotiation[8]

- Confirm your final choice[9]

1.9 NOTES ON VENUE SELECTION PROCEDURE

1. You might consider these factors:
    - Previous destinations for this event
    - Travel time and flight availability
    - Budget
    - Political and social considerations
    - Climate
    - Local levels of support
    - Local attractions
    - Your provisional programme
    - Security

2. The main categories are:
    - Resort
    - City Centre
    - Country
    - Airport

    and you may consider hotels, convention centres, heritage sites, ships, management centres or universities.

3. See List 1.10.

4. Your decision will probably be influenced by the speed and enthusiasm of the responses.

5. See List 2.2.

6. Discuss only the major financial considerations at this stage.

7. But do not make it public.

8. Discuss the minor detail of the event.

9. And communicate this decision to everyone who will be involved and to the unsuccessful venues. (Out of courtesy.)

- Short lead-times for events will often force you to condense this lengthy procedure.

1.10 A BID DOCUMENT

The search for a suitable venue cannot start until you have established exactly what you need. It will be helpful to jot down the facilities that your ideal venue must have and those which it should have. These lists will form the basis of what is termed either 'A Request for Proposals' or 'A Bid Document' to be sent to potential venues and should include:

- The title of the meeting

- The name of the organiser (with contact details)

- The type of organisation for whom it is being run[1]

- The aim of the event[2]

- A brief outline of the event[3]

- Dates and duration of the event[4]

- Maximum and minimum numbers of: delegates, partners, staff, guests, customers/clients

- The preferred location

- Details of meeting space needs (numbers of rooms, potential delegate numbers and layouts)[5]

- Details of social space needs (types of function with numbers attending, layouts, etc.)

- Details of accommodation needs per day[6]

- A programme outline

- Financial constraints[7]

- Any other vital factors[8]

1.10 NOTES ON A BID DOCUMENT

1. E.g. An explanation of who they are, e.g. Pharmaceutical Co.

2. In brief, e.g. 'to acquaint dealers with new systems'.

3. No more than one paragraph.

4. To include set up and break down time.

5. An indication of the type of A-V support being used will be helpful for space calculation purposes. Diagrams will be useful.

6. To show expected arrival and departure patterns and the mix of rooms required.

7. E.g. when a limit is placed on accommodation, or food and beverage expenditure.

8. This may be quite a long list, including such factors as:
   - recreational facilities
   - security needs
   - cultural considerations
   - disabled facilities
   - access
   - VIP participation
   - language and simultaneous interpretation.

- The Bid Document should specify which requirements are mandatory and which are only in the 'preferred' category.

- Those details which are subject to change or confirmation should also be indicated.

"In baiting a mouse trap with cheese, always leave room for the mouse"

Saki, 1924

1.11 POTENTIAL AREAS OF NEGOTIATION WITH A VENUE

As a Professional Conference Organiser, you are in a powerful position to negotiate a good deal with your chosen venue and it can be tempting to bully the management into ridiculously low room, food and beverage rates. This may make you feel good and impress your Finance Director but it will almost certainly jeopardise the vital relationship between you and the venue.

As a rule it is better to pay a reasonable rate for facilities and accommodation and then negotiate added value and service.

1. **Here are some areas of expense that you might consider asking the venue to waive or reduce.**

   - Partner rates
   - Single supplements
   - Early check in and late check out
   - Deposits
   - Meeting room charges
   - Set up and break down days
   - A-V equipment
   - Technical staff
   - Corkage charges
   - Live music
   - Use of amenities (E.g. disco, sauna etc)
   - Bar licence extension
   - Newspapers
   - Use of office equipment
   - Flowers and table settings
   - Storage facilities
   - Signs
   - Extra porters/bell staff
   - Local telephone calls
   - Parking
   - Airport transfers
   - Room for organiser after the event

2. And here are some items that you might ask the venue to include in their terms.

- Complimentary rooms
- Room upgrades
- A turn-down service
- Fruit and flowers in rooms
- Variation of payment terms
- Service charges
- Gratuities
- Cost of mains water and power
- Table furniture in meeting rooms
- Storage facilities
- Extra staff
- Continuous tea/coffee service
- Pastries with coffee
- Soft drinks
- Menu upgrade
- Wines upgrade
- Welcome cocktail
- Dry snacks
- Menu and place card printing
- Welcome letter
- Special service for VIPs
- Use of an office
- Extra bedroom amenities
- A total invoice rebate

Any conference organiser who attempts to negotiate all of the above items has totally misunderstood the concept and would be better employed as a debt collector for the Mob!

1.12 HOW TO IMPROVE THE BOTTOM LINE

Expenses and overheads can be cut by an imaginative and business-like approach to expenditure. Here are some ideas:

- Sponsorships[1]

- Adopt a flexible approach to dates and locations[2]

- Obtain three quotes for every potential service

- Consider using the printers at the destination to print programmes and on site material. This could save freight costs

- Ask the national carrier of the destination country to quote for flights

- Approach the civic authority of the destination for help[3]

- Control your hospitality expenses with a monitoring plan[4]

- Always ask all suppliers for a discount

- Use local rather than imported resources[5]

- Negotiate everything[6]

1.12 NOTES ON HOW TO IMPROVE THE BOTTOM LINE

1. Sponsors will often prefer to provide support in kind rather than cash. Conference gifts, for example, may be funded in this way.

2. Sometimes a move of a day or a few miles can provide savings of many £000s.

3. Many local authorities have funds available for civic hospitality and will offer a drinks reception. Some provide marketing support.

4. See List 1.13.

5. Gifts for example.

6. Almost everything is negotiable. See List 1.11.

A cost conscious employer invited staff to submit ideas for economies and offered a £1000 prize for the best suggestion. The first idea received said: "Cut the prize to £250".

1.13 FOOD AND BEVERAGE BUDGETS

'F & B' can be a major item of expenditure in a conference budget, so anything that can be done to reduce costs (and waste) without lowering standards, is to be welcomed. Most of the ideas on this list need a full and frank discussion with the Banqueting Manager who may not be as keen as you are to find ways to save money.

1. The Food
- Choose local ingredients in season
- Aim for perceived value on the plate[1]
- Serve smaller portions
- Smaller plates make portions seem generous
- Choose dishes where the meat or fish is chopped up[2]
- Choose dishes that provide bulk[3]
- Choose the cheaper cuts of meat[4]
- Soup is often cheaper than hors d'oeuvre[5]
- Limit the number of choices at a buffet
- Include a plain meal in the programme[6]
- For large numbers, provide continuous buffet food stations instead of lunch
- Buffets may be cheaper than waiter service
- Imaginative dainty sandwiches are better value than canapes
- Cater for fewer numbers than you have delegates[7]
- Suggest a budget to the Banqueting manager
- Consult the chef
- Negotiate a cost increase limit to the meals
- Avoid 'per drink' charging

2. The Drink
- Serve sparkling wine at receptions[8]
- Cut out the dry snacks[9]
- Choose house wines or bin ends
- Limit bar consumption on a cash basis
- Check empty wine bottles[10]
- Buy coffee/tea by the urn not per cup
- Serve iced, not bottled, water[11]
- Keep room temperatures low[12]

1.13 NOTES ON FOOD AND BEVERAGE BUDGETS

1. At the moment, items such as oysters, venison and pheasant are perceived as expensive although farming has reduced their cost.

2. Because it will go farther.

3. Pasta and pastry, for example.

4. Who will know?

5. But may take longer to serve.

6. Attendees will welcome a break from rich food.

7. You will have to pay for those delegates who always skip lunch, but a venue can cater for extras.

8. Bubbles are filling.

9. Being salty, they encourage consumption.

10. It has been known for venue staff to 'inflate' the number of bottles of wine consumed at a function. A warning that empties will be counted will normally deter such a practice.

11. Although some venues charge for this.

12. Warm people drink more.

I have served fish and chips (wrapped in the conference newspaper) to great effect, much acclaim and considerable savings.

PART TWO: PLANNING

Introduction

Now is the time to start the detailed planning. Like all complex projects, the secret is to break everything down into easily manageable components some of which you can delegate to suppliers.

At this point you will be assembling a team of people (venue staff, designers, a Destination Management Company (DMC), a speaker agency, for example) as well as your own colleagues, to create a dynamic entity with its sights set on success.

As project leader it is up to you to motivate the team and impart your enthusiasm. Good communication will be vital.

I have seen the conference organiser of a household name company assemble all the staff at his chosen venue; managers, receptionists, waiters, porters and maids to brief them about his forthcoming event and to promise them rich rewards for outstanding service. Each then received a company gift before the first delegate even arrived. He achieved the level of motivation that he sought.

Remember that professionalism is infectious. Hotel managers react very positively when they encounter an efficient (but friendly) planner.

2.1 VENUE RESEARCH

Your potential venue will mail you a comprehensive 'Conference Pack' full of useful information. Here are some of the questions it may not answer and which you should ask at an early stage:

- Which facilities will not be available over the dates in question?[1]
- When is the next refurbishment due?
- Who will be the point of contact?[2]
- What languages are spoken by staff?
- What other events are scheduled at the venue over this period?[3]
- What is the normal staff/guest ratio?[4]
- What are overtime rules for staff?
- What is the overflow policy?[5]
- What references are available?[6]
- What facilities exist for disabled delegates?
- What discount does the conference rate represent over the rack rate?
- How flexible are payment terms?
- What are the weekend rates?
- What cancellation and shortfall penalties are imposed?[7]
- What is the complimentary room policy?[8]
- How flexible is the room release schedule?
- What % commission is paid to agents?
- What is the policy on service charges, gratuities and tips?[9]
- What are the prices of popular items in bars, cafes and shops?
- What is the mark-up on telephone calls?
- How readily available are taxis at peak times?
- When are room check in/check out times?
- Are the staff union members?[10]
- What is parking capacity?

2.1 NOTES ON VENUE RESEARCH

1. Rooms and resources can be denied for all sorts of reasons – from other events/functions to refurbishment.

2. During the negotiation, during the planning and during the event.

3. Before, during and immediately after your event. Are they compatible?

4. In the venue, in the bars, in the restaurant.

5. And in which hotels? And who will pay for transfers and incidental costs?

6. It is worthwhile following up references.

7. And are they negotiable?

8. I.e. How many free rooms are on offer? (E.g. 1 per 25 or 1 per 50.)

9. Are they added after or before tax?

10. If the venue is a 'Union House' (US terminology) you may wish to see a copy of the Management/Union agreement.

"All saints can do miracles, but few of them can keep a hotel."

Mark Twain, 1835–1910

2.2 SITE INSPECTIONS

Site visits fall into three categories:

A. A Familiarisation Visit which is usually a general look at a venue or venues for future reference.

B. A Site Inspection conducted to assess the suitability of a specific venue for a specific event

C. The Liaison Visit undertaken to brief the venue on precise requirements and to discuss arrangements for a contracted event.

These lists are designed to help with 'B' above.

What to take on a site inspection:

- Two copies of the Meeting Profile
- Two copies of the Delegate profile
- Some knowledge of the destination and venue
- A provisional conference programme
- A brochure about your own organisation or that of your client
- Venue brochure and correspondence
- An area map (for marking travel times)
- A tape measure
- A room/space calculator
- A dictaphone
- A camera or camcorder
- This book
- An enquiring mind

What to bring back from a site inspection:

- The venue's Conference Pack, containing:
- Area information, maps, up to date brochure, room plans and dimensions, a plan of the venue, menus, wine lists, tariffs, staff lists
- References
- Booking conditions or a sample contract
- Social and recreational ideas
- A list of local suppliers
- CVB contacts list
- An example of the venue's usual invoice
- Photographs or film of the venue
- A visualisation of the event

2.2 NOTES ON SITE VISITS

- Time – your and the venue managers – is precious. Your will be doing everyone a favour if you have planned for your site inspection and have a clear idea what you want to see and who you wish to talk to.

- Don't be diverted into lengthy tours of facilities that are of no interest.

- Your professional approach will be noted and (hopefully) matched by the staff at the venue.

"There are two fools in every market, one who asks too little and one who asks too much"

Russian proverb

2.3 ARRANGEMENTS AT THE DESTINATION

It used to be termed 'Ground handling' but now it's been elevated to 'Destination Management'. It still means those arrangements you make to provide the best service to your attendees at the destination. Some items on this list apply only to cross-border events, others pertain anywhere away from home. Abroad, you would be well-advised to retain the services of a good Destination Management Company (DMC), au fait with local conditions, who will look after your interests.

- Customs and Immigration procedures[1]
- Baggage handling facilities[2]
- Transfer buses, taxis or limos
- Guides and couriers
- Registration services
- Inbound & outbound freight arrangements
- A local information desk
- Currency conversion arrangements
- Recreational tours and social functions .
- Off airport check-in
- Contingency plans[3]

On one of your preliminary visits to the chosen destination, you might check out the following:

- Bus standards
- Normal taxi fares
- Recreational tours
- Procedures for changing travel plans[4]
- Medical facilities
- Courier experience
- Language abilities of staff
- Who needs to be 'sweetened'
- Local protocol[5]
- Travel times[6]
- Which items attract a sales tax?[7]

2.3 NOTES ON ARRANGEMENTS AT THE DESTINATION

1. Special group arrangements can sometimes be organised.

2. Special arrangements.

3. These might include sickness, wet weather programmes, etc.

4. A % of delegates will wish to change their travel plans after arrival at the destination.

5. Who should be invited to the Conference dinner? How should the chief guest be addressed?

6. For example:
   - From flight arrival to bus departure
   - From airport to hotel
   - From hotels to meeting venue
   - From hotels to shopping areas
   - Minimum flight check-in time.

7. A DMC should be able to advise on the tax reclaim procedure.

The most compelling reason for appointing a DMC becomes apparent when there is an emergency such as a serious accident, a death, a delegate ends up in the local gaol or ... even worse ... the Chairman's golf clubs are impounded at the border.

2.4 BUDGET FOR IT – A

A checklist of items that might be included in your budget.

The Venue
Space & Time Charges
Catering
Porterage
Cloakroom facilities
Table dressing
Communication
Security
Staff costs
Press facilities
Parking
Signage
VAT/sales tax and other taxes
Service charges
Floral decoration

....

....

....

```
Setting up
Meeting rooms
Breakout rooms
Committee rooms
Conference office
Rehearsals
Exhibition
Break down
```

```
Overtime
Freelancers
Refreshments
Meals
Transport
Identification
```

Accommodation
Deposits
Bedrooms
Suites
Single supplements
Late check out
Porterage
Parking
Cancellation costs
VAT/sales tax & other taxes
Tips & Service charges
Signage
Hospitality suites
Pillow gifts
Fruit and flowers
Breakfasts
Room service
Minibars and drinks
Staff ID
Late licence
Use of health suite
Disco

....

```
V.I.P.s
Speakers
Guests
Delegates
Staff
Technicians
Interpreters
```

Extras
Coffees & teas
Telephone calls
Use of fax and photo-copier
Pager Hire

2.4 BUDGET FOR IT – B

A checklist of items that might be included in your budget.

Travel & Transport
Return fares & Transfers
Upgrades
Parking
En route costs
Signage
Baggage
Special airport facilities
Off airport facilities
Limos and car hire
Freightage
Guides & couriers
Money
Documentation
Mobile phones
Recce costs
Visas

....
....
....

Speakers
Guests
Delegates
Partners
Staff
Technicians

Airport taxes
VAT/sales tax &
other taxes
Service charges
Tips
Sweeteners

Technical
Basic equipment hire
Staging, sets & sound
systems
Electricity and water
Display materials
Interpretation &
translation
Staff
VAT/sales tax and
Customs dues
Insurance
Recordings, video &
photography
Press facilities
Exhibition material
Audience response
systems
Electronic equipment
Modems

....
....
....

Accommodation
Travel
Subsistence
(per day)
Overtime

2.4 BUDGET FOR IT – C

A checklist of items that might be included in your budget.

Social
All meals
Receptions, etc.
Speakers
Cabaret
Extra meals:
– Speakers
– Guests
– Staff
Service charges and tips
Place name cards
Seating plans
Menus/Programmes
Table dressing
Transport/transfers
Invitations
Interpreters
Security
Bad weather plan
Extra staff
Toastmaster
Signage
Cloakroom facilities
Coffees and teas
Late bar facility
Liqueurs & cigars
Wines
Dry snacks
Sound system
Lecterns
Partner programmes
Flowers
Entrance charges
Disco
Fitness facilities
Health suite
Gifts
Partner programme
....

> Travel, accommodation and meals

Printing & Design
Delegate packs
Logo etc. design
Flyer
Advertisment design & space
Mailings (incl. postage)
Registration forms
Brochure
Tickets
Programme
Menus
Daily newsletter
Press releases & packs
Review forms
Signs
Flags and Banners
Seating plans
Place cards
Badges
Sponsor lists
Location maps
Handouts
Special stationery
Welcome letter
Speech transcripts
Exhibition guide
Delegate lists
....
....

2.4 BUDGET FOR IT – D

A checklist of items that might be included in your budget.

Miscellaneous
Insurances
Recce costs
Communication ⋙⋯⋯⋯⋯⋯⋯⋙ Mobiles
Management costs
Currency exchange
Bank interest and charges
Contingency
Translation
DMC or PCO
Newspapers
Disabled facilities

....
....
....
....

> Post
> Fax
> Telephone
> Mobiles
> Pagers
> Internet

2.5 MULTI MEDIA RESOURCES

Few conferences these days do not involve the use of technology and many of the specialist suppliers whom you recruit onto your organising team will require technical support from the venue.

1. Planning
- What computer system does the venue use?[1]
- Does it use programmes for:[2]
  - layout and room design?
  - room allocation?
  - venue-wide sales records?
  - room messaging service? (TV or tel.)

2. Communications
- Which mobile phone service is available?
- Is the mobile phone service GSM
- Is mobile phone reception good throughout?
- Is there a video conferencing facility?
- Do the bedrooms have modem points
- How many telephone points are in each meeting room?
- What are the rates for telephone use?
- Can fax machines be hired for bedroom use?

3. Registration
- Does the registration area have enough power, telephone and modem points?
- Does the hotel have an emergency guest registration system?[3]

4. Presentations
- Are there any restrictions on the use of:
  - lasers?
  - infra-red systems?[4]
  - pyrotechnics?

5. General
- Is the power supply liable to surge?
- Is there an emergency power source?
- If so, does it kick in automatically?

2.5 NOTES ON MULTI MEDIA RESOURCES

1. Check on compatibility.

2. If you can plug into any of their existing systems you will save yourself much time and effort.

3. Today's reservations staff are sometimes not familiar with manual registration systems.

4. Too much ambient light in a room can degrade infra-red communication

"Modern technology
Owes ecology
An apology"

Alan Morrison, 1969

2.6 PLANNING PROGRAMMES

Many factors have to be considered when you start preparing a conference programme. The place, the people and the pennies are the most obvious and will influence what happens where and when. No list can be exhaustive but here's a start.

- What is the aim of the event?

- Where is the chosen location and what does it offer?

- What type is the venue and what facilities does it offer?

- How long is the event?

- Is it a weekday or weekend event?[1]

- Who are the attendees?[2]

- How far have they travelled?[3]

- Are delegates mainly accompanied?

- What type of programme are they accustomed to?[4]

- What is the mix of nationality?

- Is there a related exhibition?[5]

- What business sessions must be included?

- What & when are the main social events?[6]

- How interested are the audience in the subject?[7]

- What scope is there for creativity, surprise and variety?

- What are the hot topics in the industry or profession?[8]

- Which business sessions will be the most stimulating?[9]

- When are key speakers available?

- What logistic factors influence the programme?[10]

2.6 NOTES ON PLANNING PROGRAMMES

1. Sunday is still perceived as a day of rest on which a more leisurely pace is appropriate.

2. See Delegate Profile - list 1.6.

3. Consider travel fatigue, etc.

4. Choose change or conformity.

5. Time should be allowed for delegates to visit it.

6. These may be dictated by the destination or venue or speakers.

7. This may affect attendances and therefore locations.

8. These may be suitable for post-lunch sessions.

9. A mix of motivational, educational and technical sessions is preferable.

10. Consider:
    - Availability of recreational facilities
    - Registration times
    - Transfer times.

- Above all, put flexibility in your programme to allow for the unexpected which will, without doubt, occur.

"The prospect of being happy tomorrow will never console me for the boredom of today"

Student graffiti in Paris, 1968

2.7 PLANNING SOCIAL FUNCTIONS

Attendees should have cause to look forward to the social events in the programme and these should contribute to the overall objective of the event.

Here are some of the thoughts that go through my mind when I plan social functions.

- How can each function contribute to the aim of the conference?[1]

- Should we start with a low-key function or with a bang?

- Who are my delegates?[2]

- Are partners present?

- What sort of entertainment do they enjoy?

- What did they do at the last conference?

- What times are available in the business programme for social functions?[3]

- What is the best mix of large and small, informal and formal functions?

- Relaxation time is important[4]

- What sort of activities suit the location and the venue?[5]

- What facilities and resources are available on and off site?[6]

- How much can I spend on each activity or function?

- How can we involve everyone?

And it is important to remember some of the keys to a successful function ...[7]

2.7 NOTES ON PLANNING SOCIAL FUNCTIONS

1. Does it facilitate networking or re-inforce company loyalty, for example.

2. Refer to the "The Delegate Profile" list 1.6.

3. This may depend on availablity of rooms, entertainers, VIPs.

4. Allow your attendees a daily respite for them to snooze, shower, phone home, or just unwind. It is not necessary to fill every waking moment with activity.

5. Many venues have excellent 'off the peg' theme parties.

6. Some destinations offer civic hospitality in a local heritage site.

7. Such as:
   - Planned and considerate hosting of all guests, including, speakers, VIPs, supplier crews as well as delegates
   - Making invitations inviting
   - A recce of every function site
   - An original approach
   - Ice-breaking activities
   - Comprehensive briefing of venue staff
   - Rotating VIPs and celebrities around the guests
   - Avoiding queues
   - Suiting music and speaker styles to the audience.

Choose an original function venue and you're 75% home and dry. I remember arranging a picnic for 50 international delegates on a mountain top in Hong Kong overlooking the Chinese border ...

2.8 PLANNING RECREATION

The successful dovetailing of recreation and social activities into a conference programme can contribute greatly to the success of your event. Consider:

- The aim of the event
- The delegate (and partner) profile
- Time available for recreation and leisure
- What the location and venue offer
- The budget and attendees' budgets
- Achieving a balance with the professional programme
- Transfer times to recreation sites
- Climate and weather[1]
- Meals before and after recreation
- Clothing requirements
- Delegates' expectations
- Previous day's activities
- Group or individual activities
- Local factors[2]
- Availability of special equipment
- Capacities of attractions
- Travel fatigue
- Times of sunrise and sunset
- Times of important social events[3]
- Special document requirements[4]
- Disabled facilities
- Inter-site communication
- Staff availability
- Safety factors
- Insurance
- Transport requirements
- Entrance fees
- Gratuities
- Marketing and PR
- Religious or national factors
- How to ascertain numbers in advance[5]
- Contingency plans[6]
- Catering and bar facilities
- Toilets
- Storage facilities

2.8 NOTES ON PLANNING RECREATION

1. You can't do much about 'mad dogs' but Englishmen should be discouraged from going out in the midday sun.

2. All too often attendees are given leisure time when all the locals are having a siesta and the shops are closed. Also, watch out for public holidays.

3. Women may welcome hairdressing time before a formal function

4. Fitness certificates, for example.

5. If attendees are to be given a choice of recreation facilities, then an element of pre-booking will be necessary.

6. What will you do if it rains on the golf tournament?

● Much of the hassle of arranging recreation can be delegated to a professional local DMC.

I remember being involved with a function where the programme had to be changed at the eleventh hour as no-one had planned for a spring tide and the venue was inaccessible.

2.9 PLANNING MEALS

Food is an important element of a successful event so it is worth spending time and care on your 'F&B' arrangements. Luckily there are experts to advise and assist you. Here are some planning hints.

1. Who to talk to at the venue:
- The Banqueting Manager
- The Chef[1]
- The Head Waiter

2. What to ask for:
- Menus (and special diet menus)[2]
- Wine Lists
- Bar prices
- Photos of previous similar functions
- Client references
- Layout plans and capacities
- Details of off-the-peg themes

3. What to check/discuss:
- The food (appearance and taste)[3]
- The service
- Ambience and lighting
- Muzak/music (licence fees)
- Sound system and acoustics
- Disabled facilities and access
- Bar times
- Staff/attendee ratios[4]
- Staff experience/training[5]
- Breakfast (selection and speed)
- Fire exits and general security
- Location of cloakrooms & toilets[6]
- Table decor/flowers
- Hygiene (See health certificate?)[7]
- Recycling policy[8]
- Consumption controls[9]
- The price of bottled water
- Corkage charges
- Distances between rooms[10]
- The management's recommendations[11]
- Service charges and gratuities
- Local licencing laws
- The billing system
- Table sizes
- Numbers per table
- Variety[12]

2.9 NOTES ON PLANNING MEALS

1. But not just before lunch or dinner when he is at his busiest.

2. Set menus are a guide, feel free to mix and match.

3. Sample dishes that will suit your delegates.

4. E.g. ask for 1 per 50 at the bar and 1 per 10 at banquets.

5. Summer resort hotels often recruit new staff at Easter.

6. Are they large enough to cope with a rush on a wet winter's night?

7. Or ask for a walk around the kitchens.

8. Will they donate unused food to charity?

9. How does the management monitor beverage consumption?

10. I.e. How long will it take 100 people to move from the bar to the restaurant via the toilets?

11. Always take note of the suggestions of the banqueting manager and chef, they have done it all before and know what works best.

12. When all meals, on and off site, have been provisionally agreed, write them out in chronological order to ensure there is no repetition.

When overseas, beware of ethnic dishes. I once laid on a starter of squid cooked in its own ink. I was the only person to find it delicious since no-one else even tasted it.

2.10 ORGANISING ENTERTAINMENT

Stories of good conferences ruined by inappropriate entertainers are legion. The nightmares of old PCOs are filled with smutty comedians, boring after-dinner speakers and singers who are off-key.

It's a minefield out there, but these thoughts may save you from being blown up.

1. At the outset, consider:
- The Event and Delegate Profiles to decide the style of entertainment best suited to your event
- The position of the performance within the overall programme
- The venue and its facilities
- Competing attractions[1]
- The time available for the performance
- Taking the audience to the performer[2]
- Ask for the performer's references or video

2. For economy:
- Look for performers on their way up (or on their way down)
- Consider retired entertainers[3]
- Discover who is appearing elsewhere at the destination[4]
- Consider authors[5]
- Beware mega stars, they can be difficult
- Find someone to sponsor the entertainment

3. Other considerations:
- Brief the artist /or agent comprehensively[6]
- Budget for fees plus travel, accommodation and all meals. Then budget a bit more!
- Put the agreement in writing
- Insure against 'no-show'
- Be prepared to pay promptly
- Obtain permission to record all entertainment[7]
- Allow time for rehearsals
- Host performers generously
- Ask about contract 'riders'[8]

2.10 NOTES ON ORGANISING ENTERTAINMENT

1. The disco may lure away your delegates. A local concert may be a bigger draw than your chairman's speech.

2. If a super-celebrity is appearing locally, arrange to take your delegates to the show.

3. Often they will do a one-off private show.

4. They may be prepared to do a late show after their theatre performance.

5. Who may have books to sell.

6. For a big star, insist that their agent attends the performance.

7. And establish who has copyright.

8. Those 'let-out' clauses that permit an artist to break a contract.

Nursing a hangover?

"The organisation company has been corporately hospitalising a number of major clients"

Photo caption in CEII magazine

2.11 A-V SUPPORT

When you are researching the in-house audio-visual resources of a venue, here are some questions to ask.

- What in-house resources are provided?

- What technical support is available and is overtime charged?

- Does the venue operate a tied contract?

- Who is the best local supplier?[1]

- What are the costs of equipment hire?

- Is rear projection avilable?

- When are the earliest access/set up times and latest vacating time?

- What staging is available?

- What voltage is the power supply?

- Where are the power points?

- Is there a charge for use of electricity?

- What porterage and lifting equipment is available?[2]

- Where is A-V equipment normally stored and what are the security arrangements?[3]

- What sound systems are available and where are they controlled from?

- What light sources are available?

- What union regulations apply?

- What back-up equipment is available?

- Does a fire inspector have to check set ups?[4]

- Who is the technical liaison person?[5]

- Do any special local conditions apply?

2.11 NOTES ON A-V SUPPORT

1. Obtain three names and the names of past clients for reference. Give them identical briefs.

2. And are these available on a 24 hour basis and at what cost?

3. Some venues will charge for the use of storage space.

4. You may have to submit plans to the local fire inspectorate and invite a representative to visit the site. It is worth asking about local fire regulations.

5. Are they qualified?

- You should check the effectiveness of the room blackout system.

2.12 MEETING ROOM CHECKLIST

To attend a site inspection without a checklist is a recipe for extra work as vital questions will remain unasked and important features remain uninspected. Every conference brings its own demands but if you investigate the following you will be halfway there.

A. Location
- Independent access [1]
- Freight access [1]
- Easy to find? (well signed?)
- Proximity to: [2]
  - Main entrance & car park
  - Meal areas & kitchens
  - Fresh air
  - Lifts
  - Toilets & cloakrooms
  - Telephones
  - Break-out rooms
- Disabled access

B. Fixtures
- Decor
- Wall & floor materials [3]
- Pillars/obstructions
- Room shape and partitions [4]
- Location of doors
- Where doors lead to [5]
- Fire exits [6]
- Natural light/Views
- Chandeliers & mirrors [7]
- Stage area and access to it
- Registration area?
- Light switches or regulators
- Power & telephone points [8]
- Temperature controls (location) [9]
- Blackout curtains
- Acoustics
- Ceiling height [10]

C. Non fixtures
- Chairs (comfort factor)
- Tables (size & coverings)
- Table furniture [11]
- Signage

D. General
- Cleanliness
- Overall comfort
- Capacity
- Ambience
- Pre-function space
- Smell

2.12 NOTES ON MEETING ROOM CHECKLIST

1. Direct onto concourse, foyer or street.

2. Explore for yourself.

3. Should be sound absorbent, not bright and not 'busy'.

4. Are partitions really soundproof?

5. Beware doors that open onto kitchens or garbage areas.

6. Are they blocked or locked?

7. Chandeliers can impede projection. Mirrors toss light from projectors and lecterns indiscriminately around a room.

8. You may need lots for PCs, modems and fax machines.

9. Are they in the room?

10. High enough for maximum screen height.

11. What is provided? E.g. Water, cordials, note pads, mints.

Did you hear about the organiser who checked the dimensions of the access doors with the venue (over the phone) and computed that the car would fit through them? Sadly, he was unaware until the day of the launch that the room he had booked wasn't on the ground floor!

2.13 FIRE SAFETY

Following some highly publicised fires in hotels in recent years, attendees are becoming increasingly concerned about fire safety precautions. On your site inspection visit, you must ask these questions on the subject of fire safety (and then take a look for yourself.)

- What does the fire alarm sound like and who activates it?

- How often is it tested?

- When was the last fire inspection?

- When was the last fire drill?

- Are there sufficient fire extinguishers?[1]

- Are fire exits and routes, able to open, well signed and clear of obstruction?[2]

- Are fire directions posted in all rooms?

- Are bedroom doors self-closing?

- Do bedrooms have smoke detectors?

- Do the lifts automatically lock in the event of fire?

- Are room capacities posted up?

- Is there a sprinkler system throughout?

- How distant is the nearest fire station?

- Who is the venue's fire officer?

- What are the smoking regulations?

- How often are staff given fire training?

- What medical facilities are available on site and nearby?

- Are the fire instructions in English?

2.13 NOTES ON FIRE SAFETY

1. Fire extinguishers should all have labels giving the latest test date.

2. Why not try a few fire doors for yourself to see if they are locked (illegal) or obstructed?

• Local fire regulations vary from country to country and even from city to city. If you have a concern, the local Fire Department will help with advice and recommendations.

Conference centre staff rarely get the opportunity to practice fire drills with large numbers of real people. Why not offer the management your delegates for a fire practice around coffee break time?

2.14 HOTEL CONTRACT

Venue contracts are often too long, too comprehensive but, at the same time, incomprehensible. They are always drafted for the benefit of the venue not the client. Contracts will differ from event to event as your requirements change but here are some common headings.

1. Basic Conference Facts
- Agreement between .... and ....
- An agreement to ....
- Conference dates
- Estimate of numbers
- Accommodation requirements
- Meeting space requirements

2. Accommodation
- Rates
- Release dates
- Check in and out times
- Occupancy
- Complimentary rooms
- Room allocation authority

3. Meeting & Function Space
- No/type/name/dates/times
- Charges
- Release dates and penalties
- Staffing ratios
- On-site equipment & services
- Exhibition facilities

4. Food & Beverage
- Numbers for each function
- Prices & menus
- Shortfall penalties

5. Financial
- Commission rates
- Deposit arrangements
- Payment systems, dates & currencies
- Payment authorisations (who may sign)
- Charges NOT covered by contract
- Master account details

6. Miscellaneous items in the contract might include:

- Registration facilities
- Signage
- Disabled facilities
- Special requirements
- Transport
- Items negotiated into the deal
- Cancellation penalties
- Non exclusivity of the venue
- Disturbance
- Insurance & indemnity
- Safety & security
- Refurbishment 'let-out' clause
- Gratuities, taxes and service charges
- Arrangements for termination of the agreement
- Jurisdiction of the agreement
- Arbitration system
- Change of ownership

and finally ...

The dates and signatures

2.14 NOTES ON A HOTEL CONTRACT

Contracts are agreements between equals so venues do not have a monopoly on producing the contract. As a PCO you are entitled to produce your own or to delete those clauses in the venue's contract which you do not wish to sign. Remember that a verbal agreement is a binding contract.

If you create your own contract, send it to the venue prior to the venue sending their contract to you. This will strengthen your negotiating position.

"A verbal contract isn't worth the paper it's written on"

Sam Goldwyn

2.15 PREPARING THE DELEGATE

The better your attendees are briefed, the better they will understand your plans and enjoy the event that you are organising for them. That may seem obvious, but what do they really need to know?

Here is a list of **almost** everything that a participant could possibly ever want to know before attending an overseas conference.

1. About departure by air
- Which airport and which terminal
- Rendezvous point
- Earliest and latest reporting time
- Parking arrangements
- Train, bus connections
- Baggage allowances and labelling
- Baggage handling arrangements
- Details of coordinating host
- Emergency travel telephone number
- Airline
- Flight number
- Delegate recognition
- Ticket collection arrangements

2. About the flight
- What meals will be served
- Flight duration
- Type of aircraft
- Time difference to destination
- Time of arrival
- Stopover points, if any

3. Arrival and departure
- Reception arrangements
- Baggage arrangements
- Transfers
- Money changing facilities
- Passport, Visa, etc. controls
- Hotel, name address and tel. no.
- Details of DMC or equivalent
- Return flight details
- Customs allowances (out and in)

4. About the Destination

- A brief on the country or region
  (Politics, culture, history etc.)
- Climate, weather and temperatures
- Hotel brief (facilities)
- Host staff names
- Local do's and dont's
- Dress code or guidance
- Details of local handling agents
- Address of local Consulate
- Travel insurance requirements
- Language
- Currency
- Local taxes (esp. on departure)
- Electrical voltage and socket type
- Availability and proximity of basic services
  e.g. banks, hairdressers, drug stores, etc.
- Details of churches and services
- Local transport guidance
- Health hazards and innoculations
- Passport and visa requirements
- Facilities for the disabled and children
- A local 'What's On' diary
- Shop opening hours
- Local attractions guide
- Tipping policy
- How to telephone home
- Crime threat and security guidance
- Map of locality or city

5. About the Conference

- Conference title
- Host organisation
- Business programme
- Partner programme
- Social programme
- Interpretation facilities
- Badging policy
- Pre and post conference tours
- Registration times and place
- Organising committee
- Sponsors
- What is included in the conference fee?

PART THREE: ON SITE

Introduction

The months of knitting the different strands together into a complete tapestry are over. Everything is in place. Your team are ready to go into action to create a transcendent event. If your marketing has been effective, the participants will be looking forward to the conference as much as you are.

Before you travel to the conference venue (at least 24 hours prior to the first arrivals) take the time to stand back and, like a general before an engagement, survey the battlefield. Anything that is not in place by now, probably never will be. It is too late for new ideas. Avoid the temptation to involve yourself with the minutiae; leave that to someone else in the team. Don't give yourself mundane tasks that may prevent you from monitoring the big picture.

This is your event. Your reputation is on the line so, at this point, you become senior problem solver - occasionally, senior crisis manager. It is vital that you are able to take a strategic view as the days unfold according to your master plan.

One word of advice. Don't be tempted to go around asking the delegates what they think of the conference. You will inevitably encounter Mr. Dissatisfied who will ruin your day and dent your self-confidence. If he, or any others, feel really aggrieved, they will seek you out.

3.1 THE DECISION HEDGEHOG

Your ideas may be exciting and your plans painstaking but unless you communicate them to everyone involved they are worthless. Here is an attempt to list all those people and organisations that may need to know every time you take a decision.

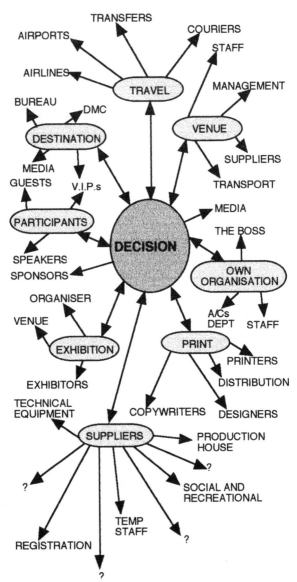

3.1 NOTES ON THE DECISION HEDGEHOG

- Experienced event planners will tell you that nothing is firm until it is in writing. The trouble is that even written confirmation cannot ensure compliance.

  Letters get lost, faxes can disappear into a black hole in the ether and memos end up in the wrong tray.

  I believe in the principle of the three Rs:

  RING
  (W)RITE
  REMIND

3.2 DELEGATE REGISTRATION

Whoever invented the computer must have been responsible for convention registration in a previous existence. The micro chip was made for the task of registration. Here are a few suggestions to make this vital operation as hassle-free as possible.

In advance
- Encourage pre-registration[1]
- Design simple, idiot-proof forms
- Ask a colleague to complete each of your forms to ensure they are delegate-friendly
- Make your forms attractive so that delegates want to complete them immediately on receipt[2]
- Consider early registration incentives
- Consider late-booking penalties
- Encourage credit card payment
- Send out badges in advance
- Utilise the Internet for pre-registration

On site
- Employ about one staffer per 50 delegates
- Brief staff fully
- Use multiple registration booths[3]
- Deter cash payment (but have receipt books ready)
- Display clear and comprehensive signs[4]
- Remember security (people and cash)
- Consider cloakroom needs[5]
- Consider computerising the registration function[6]
- Segregate VIP, staff, supplier, and media check in points
- Employ floating (trouble shooter) staff
- Set up a special service/check in point[7]
- Consider distractions and entertainments at potential queue points
- Reserve a private, central area for your staff and storage needs

3.2 NOTES ON DELEGATE REGISTRATION

1. This also acts as a useful advance indicator about levels of interest.

2. Forms can even be fun.

3. These are best alphabetised for those who have registered in advance and are only picking up a badge or signing in.

4. Signs should be above head level.

5. A cloakroom located before registration may ease congestion, if it is fully staffed.

6. For events of more than 500 a computerised system is a necessity.

7. Any registration query that isn't quick and straightforward should be referred to the special service desk so as to avoid holding up the flow.

- Remember that you will need a large surface to lay out badges.

- Registration is the delegates' first impression of the event and of your organisation. It should be friendly, simple, quick and queue-free.

"Americans wear name badges because they like to proclaim themselves. The British don't because they wish to pass un-noticed"

Anon

3.3 ROOM LAYOUTS

In planning the layout of a meeting room there are principles and there are local considerations. These lists suggest some planning factors you may wish to take into account.

Theatre Style

- Place chairs facing the long side of the room

- The front row of chairs should be no more than 4m (13ft) and no less than 2m (6.5ft) from the front of the stage

- Place chairs in an ellipse, (not in straight rows), facing the stage

- Aisles and lanes should be at least 2m (6.5ft) wide

- Avoid having a centre aisle

- Allow .75 sqm (8 sqft) per person

- A rough and ready formula is:-
  Audience numbers x 2.5 = space required in sqm plus 50% for stage and walkways

- The front row of chairs should not be less than twice the screen height from the screen

- The back row of chairs should not be more than eight times the screen height from the screen

Classroom Style

- Layout as for theatre style but allow 1.5 sqm (16 sqft) per person to accommodate tables/desks

Other Styles

- For meetings of a more participatory nature, choose between U shape, hollow square, board-room, E or T shape, herring bone or cafe (cabaret) style

3.3 NOTES ON ROOM LAYOUTS

- Suit the layout to the aim of the function.

- Take a very flexible approach to these figures when a room doesn't conform to the rectangular or there are obstructions.

- Beware the extra space demands of rear projection.

- Enquire about local fire safety regulations that may demand wider aisles or pools of space around fire exits and the front of the stage.

- Ask the venue to lay out the room as you would like to see it ... and then count capacity.

- Remember the needs of the disabled, e.g. special areas for wheel chairs or the hard of hearing.

- Don't be reluctant to turn a layout around to suit a presentation.

- Beware retractable raked seating, it can be noisy to walk on.

- Tables should always be draped (individually) but not on the seat side.

- Meeting Professionals International (MPI) stocks a useful space ready reckoner (see Appendix page 87).

Bear in mind that venue managers rarely attend conferences in their own meeting rooms so they do not have to suffer the layouts as prescribed in their brochure or the discomfort of their chairs.

3.4 BASIC AUDIO-VISUAL AIDS

A surprising number of seasoned presenters will turn to the meeting planner for help when the lamp on the overhead projector goes out. Some technical equipment should be left to the technicians, but a PCO should know how to operate the basic A-V aids.

The basic equipment used by presenters is:

- The Whiteboard
- The Flip Chart and stand[1]
- The Overhead Projector[2]
- The Video Cassette Recorder[3]
- The 35mm Slide projector[4]
- A simple sound system[5]

A working knowledge of these is within the domain of the PCO. This includes:

- capabilities and characteristics
- simple fault finding
- operation
- access to spare equipment and parts

It is also important for the PCO to understand the relationship between focal lengths, screen sizes and visibility in an auditorium:

- The base of the screen and the projector should be more than 1.5m (6. ft) above the floor
- Screen width should be one and a half times screen height, for slides & OHP
- The front row should not be less than twice the height of the screen away from it
- The back row should not be more than eight times the height of the screen away from it
- Ceiling height should be more than 3.5m (11ft) high

'Front projection' is when the projector is on the audience side of the screen and 'rear projection' is when it is behind the screen.[6]

3.4 NOTES ON BASIC AUDIO-VISUAL AIDS

1. This workhorse has humbled many confident presenters, check it for:
   - stability
   - tight screws
   - properly fastened paper
   - unused pads
   - pens which write
   - visibilty from all parts of the room.

2. Problems can include:
   - 'keystoning' (a distorted image)
   - dead spare bulb
   - dirty or scratched platen
   - too low wattage
   - the OHP itself obscuring vision
   - screen too low.

3. Establish which format is needed. Systems are sometimes incompatible.

4. It is important to know:
   - How to switch it on and off
   - How to focus
   - How the remote operates
   - How to change a bulb
   - How to mount the carousel
   - Which way to place the slides in the magazine or carousel
   - Which slide mounts are best
   - How to prevent condensation on slides.

5. It is helpful to know about microphone types and their uses.

6. Different screens are used for rear and front projection. They are not interchangeable.

Obtain one of the many excellent users guides to Audio-Visual equipment (produced free by the major manufacturers).

3.5 SPEAKERS BRIEF

Your guest speakers need to know as much about your conference as the delegates do and more. Here are some headings to include in a Speakers Brief.

- Title of event and host organisation
- His/her personal contact, with direct line telephone and fax numbers
- The aim of the conference
- The purpose of the speaker's talk[1]
- The dates of the Conference
- The venue (address, tel., fax nos, etc.)
- The time of the speakers appearance
- The Delegate Profile[2]
- Likely numbers in the audience
- What is expected of the speaker. E.g:
    - Topic and treatment
    - Duration
    - Presentation format
- What sessions precede and succeed his/her appearance
- The speaker fee and payment method
- What expenses are covered[3]
- What A-V facilities are available
- What interpretation facilities are being provided in which languages
- The details of distribution of papers[4]
- Details of media coverage[5]
- Travel arrangements
- Accommodation details
- Social event invitations
- Any VIP involvement
- The timetable of communication with the speaker
- Latest dates by which material is needed[6]
- Details of other speakers and their topics
- Whether the speaker will be evaluated
- Background on the host organisation
- Dress code

3.5 NOTES ON SPEAKERS BRIEF

1. How it fits into the programme.

2. See list 1.6.

3. Be specific to avoid later embarrassment.

4. Explain the system.

5. I.e. will the media be present?

6. E.g. papers, extracts, slides etc.

- Repeat the title of the speaker's session in each correspondence.

- Your speakers may find all this more digestible if it is divided into two mailings.

- These headings can become the meat of a contract.

- A hidden purpose of this comprehensive brief is to demonstrate your professionalism to the speaker and to imply that you expect it to be matched!

"It usually takes me more than three weeks to prepare a good impromptu speech"

Mark Twain

3.6 FUNCTION REQUIREMENT FORM

Every function or session within your conference programme should be treated as a unique event. Each demands its own instructions so that everyone involved is fully briefed. The following are examples of what you might include in a Function Requirement Form.

- This event/function is part of ...

- Title of event/function

- Aim of event/function

- Planner contact numbers: room, pager, mobile phone, etc.

- Date

- Times:
  - Set up
  - Start
  - End
  - Venue Free

- Venue (room) name

- Layout – draw a plan

- Attendance numbers

- VIP names

- Who are attendees

- Materials needed:
  - Table - pads, place cards, pencils, water, mints, etc.
  - Furniture - lecterns, spare chairs, pointer
  - Colour scheme - table dressing
  - Signs - at reception/room
  - Flower arrangements

- A-V Requirements
  - 35 mm projector
  - Carousel trays
  - OHP
  - Screen(s)
  - Blackboard
  - Whiteboard } With markers
  - Flip charts
  - TV monitor and VCR
  - Other equipment
  - Blackout
  - Dimmer lighting
  - Telephone
  - Stand mic(s)
  - Table mic(s)
  - Tie (lavaliere) mic(s)
  - Radio mic(s)
  - Extension cords
  - Cassette player
  - Radio
  - Modem points

- Session times
  - Assemble
  - First break
  - Second break } Beverages required
  - Third break
  - Dispersal

- Food Requirements (special diets)
  - Menu
  - Beverages

- Reception and Staffing
  - (Reception/Registration, Porterage)
  - Planning staff
  - Venue staff

- Special Requirements
  - Security - for VIPs, equipment
  - Deliveries - equipment, exhibits
  - Billing format

Your venue should also provide you with a similar form confirming the arrangements they have made. It is sensible to cross-check their brief against yours.

3.7 RISK AND CRISIS MANAGEMENT

Few professionals in the event management business approach their work confident that everything will go exactly according to plan and without a hitch. Experience has taught us that Murphy's law is as prevalent in our field as any other and we find it reassuring to have contingency plans.

1. Risk management
- Catalogue the possible risks to:[1]
  - The event as a whole
  - The delegates
  - The speakers and VIPs
  - The venue
  - The travel plans
  - The organisers

- Assess the likelihood of each hazard

- Assess the potential damage[2]

- Consider the following types of emergency:
  - Medical[3]
  - Personal safety[4]
  - Security[5]

- Consider what you can do to minimise these risks. For example:
  - Staff training & briefing
  - Utilising local resources[6]
  - Establishing special procedures
  - Inspecting areas of concern
  - Rehearsing emergency drills
  - Setting up communications[7]
  - Insurance

2. Crisis Management
- When the unforeseen happens (the foreseen is not a crisis):
  - Obtain accurate information ASAP
  - Take advice from experts[8]
  - Take time to make a decision[9]
  - Brief staff
  - Communicate & lead[10]

3.7 NOTES ON RISK AND CRISIS MANAGEMENT

1. Risks have either natural causes (e.g. the weather) or human (deliberate or accidental) causes.

2. Damage may be caused to people, places, reputations or objectives.

3. Such as food poisoning, heart attacks, etc.

4. Such as unsafe scaffolding, fire.

5. Such as the threat of kidnap or riot.

6. Health inspectors, police.

7. Always have an up-to-date, local, emergency contact list.

8. E.g. local police, doctor, venue executives, etc.

9. Never rush to a conclusion, a considered decision will be a better solution.

10. Make sure that everyone who needs to know what is happening and what is going to happen, has been told. Don't forget to brief the media.

As the event organiser you have a duty of care to your delegates and a leadership responsibility. When things go wrong the buck stops with you. Don't dodge it.

PART FOUR: POST CONFERENCE

Introduction

By this stage, you are blushing from all the compliments you have received for running such a successful conference. Enjoy them while they last. In a few days you will be forgotten and your event will be only a pleasant memory. "We are" the cliché says, "only as good as our last success."

It is a good idea, therefore, to extract the last drops of nectar from the fading blossom before it wilts and dies. Encourage participants to put their praise in writing. Ask the Venue manager to drop a complimentary line to your CEO. Get those photographs taken of you and the celebrity speaker!

And don't forget the other members of your successful team. They also need to hear the plaudits and receive the compliments. Be generous in your praise and sparing in your criticism. (If criticise you must, leave it for a few days.)

4.1 POST CONFERENCE REPORT

And just when you thought you could relax ... there's a report to write.

Experience and circumstances will dictate what you might include but here are some ideas:

- General comments [1]

- Basic details of the event [2]

- Basic details of the venue [3]

- Details of any related exhibition

- Attendance statistics [4]

- Average length of stay

- Total room nights with breakdown [5]

- Function numbers & shortfall [6]

- Session attendances

- Recreation take up

- Payment records [7]

- Actual cash flow report

- List of suppliers [8]

- List of sponsors

- Profit/Loss statement

- Budget analysis (forecast/actual)

- Recommendations for the future

- Summary of achievement [9]

4.1 NOTES ON POST CONFERENCE REPORT

1. Include your opinions about every aspect of the event and perhaps a summary of the delegates' evaluation forms. Did they enjoy it?

2. Who, what , when, where, why, etc.

3. Address, tel/fax, contact name, etc.

4. How many: delegates, partners, staff, speakers, VIPs, no shows etc.

5. Divide into singles, twins, suites and list by attendees above. This is vital for planning a possible repeat event.

6. How many and who attended the social events, meals, etc. Compare with planning figures.

7. Which delegates paid promptly and which didn't.

8. Were they good, bad or indifferent? A relevant note will help you and/or your successor.

9. State whether you achieved the aim of the event.

"Never write what you dare not say."

English proverb

4.2 AFTER THE EVENT

"It's not over till the fat lady sings" they say, but a conference is not over even then ... for the organiser. All this needs to be done!

- Discuss the event with venue management

- Tip venue staff - if appropriate [1]

- Hold a post mortem meeting

- Analyse the delegate evaluation forms

- Check accounts

- Send out press releases & transcripts

- Follow up on photography, etc.

- Pay all invoices promptly [2]

- Solicit quotes from attendees [3]

- Write and thank all contributors [4]

- Compile and circulate a Post Conference Report [5]

- Reconcile your budget

- Compile an archive file on the event

- Start a 'Future' file if the event is likely to be staged again

- Distribute relevant photographs, videos, press cuttings, etc. to the venue

- Thank and reward your project team [6]

- Ask: "Have I achieved the conference objective?"

- Take a holiday (see opposite)

4.2 NOTES ON AFTER THE EVENT

1. A contentious subject, ask the venue manager for advice.

2. Don't get a reputation as a slow payer.

3. These may be used to promote the following year's event.

4. Venue, suppliers, speakers, airlines, the local CVB, etc.

5. See list 4.1.

6. Throw a party, buy them flowers, take them to the theatre. They deserve the credit as much as you do!

• Evaluation of the event is vital, MPI offers a self-learning module entitled "Return on Investment".

A PCO of my acquaintance has it written into her contract that she will remain at the venue for two days after a major event to relax, unwind ... and check the accounts.

APPENDICES

1. Useful Addresses and Contacts

2. Glossary of General Terms

APPENDIX 1

USEFUL ADDRESSES AND CONTACTS

INTERNATIONAL
Asian Association of Convention and Visitor Bureaus (AACVB)
AACVB Secretariat, C/o Macau Government Tourist Office, Largo Do Senado, No 9 PO Box 3006 Macau
Tel: + 853 338 084 Fax: + 853 510104

Association Internationale des Interpretes de Conference
10, Avenue de Secheron, 1202 Geneva, Switzerland
Tel: + 41 22 908 15 40 Fax: + 41 22 732 41 51
e:mail 100665.2456@compuserve.com

Association Internationale des Palais De Congres
AIPC 6 Rue du Musee, B-1000 Brussels, Belgium
Tel: +32 2 522 5094 Fax: +32 2 522 5094

European Federation of Conference Towns
BP 182B, 1040 Brussels, Belgium
Tel: +32 2 732 6954 Fax: +32 2 735 4840
e:mail efct@pophost.evnet.be

International Association of Professional Congress Organisers
40 rue Washington, 1050 Brussels, Belgium
Tel: +32 2 640 71 05 Fax: +32 2 640 4731
e:mail iapco@pophost.evnet.be

International Congress & Convention Association
Entrada 121, 1096 EB Amsterdam, Netherlands
Tel: +31 20 690 1171 Fax: +31 20 699 0781
e:mail icca@icca.nl

Meeting Professionals International
European Bureau, Bld St Michel 15, B1040, Brussels, Belgium
Tel: + 32 2 743 1544 Fax: + 32 2 743 1550

Meetings Industry Association of Australia (MIAA)
P O Box 380 Spit Junction, NSW 2088 Australia
Tel: + 61 9969 1400 Fax: + 61 29969 2856

UNITED STATES

International Association of Convention and Visitor Bureaux

2000 l St NW Suite 702, Washington DC 20036-4990 USA
Tel: + 1 202 296 7888 Fax: + 1 202 296 7889
e:mail gbarrett@iacvb.org
WWW: http://www.iacvb.org

Meeting Professionals International

4455 LBJ Freeway, Suite 1200, Dallas, Texas 75244-5309
USA
Tel: + 1 214 702 3000 Fax: + 1 214 702 3070
Web site: http://www.mpiweb.org

UNITED KINGDOM

Association of Exhibition Organisers

26 Chapter Street, London, SW1P 4ND
Tel: +44 (0) 171 932 0252 Fax: +44 (0) 171 932 0299

Association for Conferences and Events

ACE International, Riverside House, High Street,
Huntingdon, Cambs PE118 6SG
Tel: +44 (0) 1480 457595 Fax: +44 (0) 1480 412863

Association of National Tourist Organisations

Studio 101, Mill Studios, Crane Mead, Ware,
Herts SG12 9PY
Tel: +44 (0) 1920444 243 Fax: +44 (0) 1920 444 246
e:mail coplus@coplus.demon.co.uk

British Association of Conference Destinations

1st Floor, Elizabeth House, 22 Suffolk Street, Queensway,
Birmingham B1 1LS
Tel: +44 (0) 121 616 1400 Fax: +44 (0) 121 616 1364

British University Accommodation Consortium

University Park, Nottingham NG7 2RD
Tel: +44 (0) 115 950 4571 Fax: +44 (0) 115 942 2505

British Tourist Authority and English Tourist Board

Business Travel Department, Thames Tower,
Black's Road, Hammersmith, London W6 9EL
Tel: + 44 (0) 181 563 3252 Fax: +44 (0) 181 563 3153

Corporate Hospitality Association

Arena House, 66–68 Pentonville Road, Islington, London N1 9HS

Tel: +44 (0) 171 278 0288 Fax:+ 44 (0) 171 837 5326

Incentive Travel & Meetings Association

P O Box 195, Twickenham, Middlesex RW1 2PE

Tel: + 44 (0) 181 892 0256 Fax: +44 (0) 181 891 3855

Meetings Industry Association

34 High Street, Broadway, Worcs WR12 7DT

Tel: +44 (0) 1386 858572 Fax: +44 (0) 1386 858986

APPENDIX 2

GLOSSARY OF GENERAL TERMS

Action Schedule
Document listing all actions that need to be completed to ensure the success of an event and including the person or organisation responsible for each and the date by which they should be completed. Business Plan.

Audio-Visual (A-V)
Generic term covering the technical materials and methods used to support communication with an audience by visual or aural means.

Bid Document
Document containing details of a planned event requesting venues to bid to host it. Request for Proposal or Bid Manual.

Bottom Line
Jargon for the final financial profit or loss of a project.

Break-down time
Time allocated for the dismantling and removal of conference or exhibition structures. (Tear-down time)

Carriers
Companies in the business of transporting people and goods. Mainly used for airlines.

Conference destination
The locality where an event may be held.

Conference Pack
A pack of printed (and sometimes video or CD ROM) material designed to promote a venue and comprehensively brief prospective users.

Corkage
A per bottle cost charged by an establishment when customers bring their own beverages.

Courier
A person employed to supervise and escort tours and groups. A steward.

CVB
Convention and Visitor Bureau. (US and increasingly Europe). Also 'Office of Tourism', etc. for a city, locality or region.

DDR
Daily Delegate Rate. An inclusive per delegate charge by the venue. 24 hour rate is meeting facilities plus full board. 12 hour rate is meeting facilities plus lunch and refreshments.

Delegate
A generic term for people who attend the business sessions of a meeting whether or not they have been delegated to do so. (US = attendee)

Delegate Profile
A short document outlining the common characteristics of the people attending an event, for the information of all involved.

DMC
Destination Management Company. (Previously known as a 'Ground Handling Agent') A company offering local knowledge and organisational assistance at the destination.

Economy
The basic class of travel with an airline. (US = Coach).

Enhancements
Those items and activities added to a basic conference to make it more interesting, enjoyable or unusual.

F & B
Food and Beverage

Flyer
A one page printed notice promoting an event.

Late licence
Special licence issued by a liquor licensing authority for an establishment to continue selling alcohol beyond the normal permitted hours

Meeting Profile
A short document outlining the objective and basic elements of an event for the information of all involved. A Brief.

Meeting space
The areas in a venue where the business sessions of a meeting will take place

Murphy's Law
This states that if anything can go wrong, it will.

OHP
Overhead Projector.

Partner
An accompanying person who is a guest of a delegate. Not necessarily a spouse and sometimes referred to as 'a significant other'. (US)

Pass Throughs
Items of expenditure passed on to a client by an agency without a % add-on.

PCO
Professional Conference Organiser. Meeting Planner (US). May be employed within an organisation or be an independent freelance

Podium
Stage for presenters

Production company
A company which creates and stages the presentation elements of a conference or product launch. It may also undertake to provide a theme for an event.

Rack Rate
The published tariff for a hotel bedroom.

Recce
Reconnaissance

Registration
The procedure of accepting someone as a delegate to an event. This may be carried out in advance and/or on site.

Review form
A form for attendees to complete which seeks their views on aspects of the event. A research tool.

RV
Rendezvous or Meeting point.

Single Supplement
An addition to the daily tariff charged by a hotel when a double room is occupied by only one person.

Social space
The areas of a venue where the social activities related to a conference will take place

Staging
1) n. Components used to create a temporary stage. Risers (US).
2) v. The act of putting on a show or presentation.

Stake-holders
Those people or organisations with a stake in the successful outcome of an event. Eg. sponsors, delegates, suppliers, etc.

Subsistence allowance
Paid to some freelance staff for periods away from home. (Sometimes in lieu of expenses)

Suppliers
Those people and organisations who provide equipment, facilities or services to the event organiser.

Sweeteners
Known in some circles as bribes.

Syndicate sessions
Small group meetings within the conference. Break-out sessions (US).

Total invoice rebate
A negotiated agreement whereby the supplier (usually the venue) agrees to pay the buyer a % rebate if the total spend is more than an agreed figure.

Transfers
Travel industry jargon for the movement of people between airports/harbours/rail stations and hotels/venues.

Turn down service
Hotel shorthand for the service of turning down beds in the evening.

Upgrades
Those passengers whom airlines seat in a better class than that paid for.

VAT
Value added tax. A variable purchase tax imposed on most goods and services in Europe. Recoverable in some circumstances.

Venue
A place where a meeting is held. Site (US).

VIP
Very Important Person.

VCR
Video Cassette Recorder (or VTR – Video Tape Recorder).